D1398526

EXCITING
thailand
a visual journey

Welcome to Thailand,
Land of Grace and Beauty

PERIPLUS

EXCITING
thailand

F EW COUNTRIES PROVIDE a warmer or more entrancing welcome than Thailand. It's a kingdom that has just about everything. The pristine beaches of Phuket, Ko Samui and the south are legendary, as is the mouth-watering cuisine. The far north of the country is home to a dozen different colourful hill tribes and is an ideal setting for trekking, elephant-riding and white water rafting. The little-known east of the country boasts a string of jewel-like Khmer temples. Then there's Bangkok, the nation's capital, known to the Thais as the "City of Angels"—one of the most vibrant and exciting cities in the world, packed with cultural treasures, fine hotels, great restaurants and a nightlife that is unsurpassed.

20 Sukhothai

THAILAND

Thais are famous for their friendliness and sense of fun. *Sawasdee* means hello in Thai and *sanuk*—another essential word—means fun or enjoyment!

sawasdee!

tHAILAND means "Land of the Free"—and with reason, for despite withstanding various invasions from neighbouring Myanmar and, most recently, Japan, the country has never been colonised. The first independent Thai kingdom was founded in the mid-12th century by King Ramkhamhaeng the Great at Sukhothai in the north-central plains. By the 17th century the Thai capital had moved south, to Ayutthaya, and Thailand was established as an important maritime trading power.

Left: Wat Phra Keo, at the centre of the Royal Palace complex on Rattanakosin Island in downtown Bangkok, lies at the heart of the ruling Chakri Dynasty and of the Thai kingdom itself.
Above: Thai dancers, wearing *lep yao* or "long fingernails", display the smiles for which the kingdom is famous.

Clockwise from top:
Traditional stilt house
above the waters of the
Chao Phraya River.
Harvesting rice on the broad
plateau of northeast Thailand.
Floating houses on the river
at Uthai Thani.
A display of baskets for sale
at a local market.
Planting rice in the rich
central plains.
Facing page: Mahouts riding
elephants near Mae Hong
Song in northern Thailand.

In 1767 Ayutthaya was sacked by invading
Burmese armies in a major military setback for
Thailand. Yet this was a mixed blessing, for within
20 years the resilient Thais had re-established themselves under the powerful Chakri Dynasty, and had
begun the building of a new capital at Bangkok, the
"Olive Tree Village", later renamed Krungthep, or
"City of Angels". Alone of the countries in Southeast Asia, Thailand retained independence throughout the colonial period and emerged relatively un-
scathed from World War II. Under the benign rule
of King Bhumibol Adulyadej—currently the longest
reigning monarch in the world—the country has
continued to flourish, emerging as a leading and
increasingly prosperous Southeast Asian nation.

thai buddhism

Although many religions are practised in Thailand, Theravada Buddhism—the "Way of the Elders"— is the bond that has held the nation together and identified the nature of "Thai-ness".

Facing page: Gilded figures of the Lord Buddha abound throughout the kingdom.
Clockwise from far left:
Buddhist monks on their early morning alms round.
Detail of a gilded stupa at Doi Suthep, Chiang Mai.
Monks at a temple near Bangkok during Makha Bucha celebrations.
Portrait of a venerated monk at a Thai temple.

ABOUT 90 PER CENT of Thais are Buddhists, most of them devout in their belief. Until King Bhumibol Adulyadej ascended the throne in 1946, Buddhism was perceived as the religion of the kingdom—indeed, the definition of being Thai was to be Buddhist, a monarchist, and to speak the Thai language, *phasaa tai*. In practice, this still holds true today. But under the wise guidance of King Bhumibol, and in line with the rapid growth of democracy in the kingdom, recognition is now fully given to the minority religions—Christianity, animism amongst the hill tribes of the north, Hinduism, and above all Islam, Thailand's second religion, dominant in the southern provinces.

bangkok

"To Bangkok! Magic name, blessed name!"
from Joseph Conrad, *Youth*.

Facing page:
Bangkok at dawn.
Clockwise from far left:
A tuk-tuk, Thailand's unique contribution to personal urban transport.
Heavy traffic is characteristic of the "City of Angels".
Condominiums and palaces of business loom over the Chao Phraya, the "River of Kings".
The Silom Road area, Bangkok's financial centre.
Modern building in down-town Bangkok.

bANGKOK WAS ESTABLISHED as the capital of Thailand by King Rama I, founder of the Chakri Dynasty, in 1782. Once known as the "Venice of the East" because of its extensive network of canals, it has today grown into a bustling megalopolis, one of the largest cities in the Far East. Yet despite its size, Bangkok is a city of great charm and many different faces. Behind the glass and concrete towers of Silom Road, the city's Wall Street, and beneath the sleek, new elevated skytrain and gleaming shopping malls lie many oases of peace and calm where traditional, Thai-style wooden houses are reflected in tranquil, lotus-filled ponds. It's a city that takes a while to get to know, but which very soon finds a permanent place in the visitor's heart.

King Rama I built Bangkok on the east bank of the great Chao Phraya River as a protection against Burmese attack and to facilitate maritime trade with Europe and the Far East.

Today much of Bangkok is comprised of modern, high-rise buildings served by a network of raised expressways, but the heart of Rama I's city, known as Rattanakosin Island, retains many original 18th- and early 19th-century temples and palaces, and is still served by a network of canals.

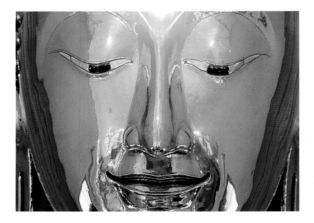

Clockwise from above: Serene features of the Golden Buddha at Wat Traimit, Bangkok.
Elaborate gilded decoration at the Royal Palace, Bangkok.
Thai nuns outside the Marble Temple, Bangkok.
Facing page, clockwise from top: Wat Arun illuminated at dusk.
Slender chedis at Wat Pho.
Head of the reclining Buddha at Wat Pho.
Interior of the late 18th-century Wat Buddhaisawan.

It would be difficult to overestimate the feelings of loyalty and esteem in which the Thais hold both their religion, Buddhism, and their monarch, King Bhumibol. Indeed loyalty to the monarchy—which is closely associated with the Buddhist religion—dates back at least as far as King Ramkhamhaeng of Sukhothai (1279–1298), whilst King Chulalongkorn, the fifth of the Chakri monarchs (1868–1910) is so greatly revered that he has become a national symbol of morality and renewal.

Facing page: Devout worshippers making offerings at Bangkok's Wat Phra Kaew.
Top: King Bhumibol Adulyadej, ninth monarch of the Chakri Dynasty.
Middle, left: Central Throne Hall, Royal Palace, Bangkok.
Middle, right: Eastern Gallery of the Royal Palace with murals of the Kings of the Chakri Dynasty.

Above: Interior of the Royal Palace, Bangkok.
Right: Royal Barge Ceremony on the Chao Phraya River, Royal Palace in the background.

Facing page: Passengers in a long-tail boat sail past an elaborate temple landing.
Clockwise from top: Barges on the Chao Phraya River near central Bangkok. Passengers on a canal boat by a village in the Central Plains. Covered boats wait for passengers by a hotel terrace, downtown Bangkok. Long-tail boat speeding along a *klong* (canal) in Thonburi.

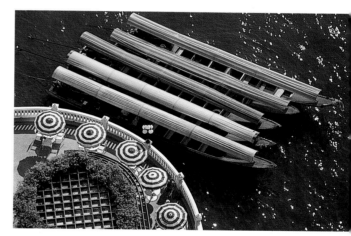

Although no longer simply a city of canals, much of Bangkok's life still revolves around its many waterways, from the great Chao Phraya River to the winding canals, or *klongs*, of Thonburi. Noisy, long-tail boats speed hither and thither carrying all manner of small cargo and passengers, many of them commuters using the canals as a way of circumventing the capital's notorious traffic. Great lines of barges, sometimes as many as six in a row, carry rice or oil up and down the river, whilst small children splash in the narrows near their back porches and old men sit mending fishing nets or simply watching the world go by.

the floating market

In central and southern Thailand, water-borne commerce is as old as time.

Clockwise from top: Women dominate trade at Thailand's floating markets.
A string of covered barges on a canal in Ratchaburi.
Catching fish at Damnoen Saduak.
Fresh chillis and other vegetables displayed on a boat at Damnoen Saduak floating market.
Facing page: Traders at a floating market accrue merit by giving offerings of food to a passing monk.

Much of Thailand's commerce has traditionally been carried out on the nation's many rivers and waterways. Although today this custom is in decline, especially in the large cities, floating markets still exist—most notably at Damnoen Saduak in Ratchaburi Province to the southwest of Bangkok. A visit to one of Thailand's floating markets is a must for any visitor, but to see them at their colourful, bustling best it is essential to set out early, as most trading takes place just after sunrise.

Clockwise from top: The three Khmer-style temple towers of Wat Si Sawai.
The red brick stupa of Wat Chetuphon at Sukhothai.
Wat Phra Si Ratana at Chaliang is a revered Sukhothai monument.
Facing page: Lotus-filled pond in front of 13th-century Wat Mahathat, Sukhothai's largest temple.

sukhothai

Capital of the first independent Thai kingdom, the tranquil ruins of Sukhothai have become a potent symbol of pride in the hearts of all Thais.

Thais are justifiably proud of Sukhothai, a central symbol of Thai nationhood. For this reason they have gone to a great deal of trouble to restore the ruins at Sukhothai, as well as at the neighbouring related sites of Sri Satchanalai and Kamphaeng Phet. Today the historical parks that surround these once-bustling cities are immaculately kept, and set off the monuments to great effect. Sukhothai is traditionally regarded as the home of Thailand's lovely Loy Krathong Festival, where elaborate floats bearing flowers, candles, incense and a coin are floated on rivers and waterways. For lovers, especially, this is an important festival—if two krathongs released at the same time float away together, the relationship will prosper and the couple stay together!

Clockwise from top:
Pensive monk at Wat Si Chum.
Wat Mahathat at sunset.
Loy Krathong at Sukhothai. This festival takes place each November at the time of the full moon.
Elaborate Loy Krathong float.
Parade at Loy Krathong Festival.
Facing page: Sukhothai illuminated for Loy Krathong festivities.

Above: Sunset over the Gulf of Thailand at Rayong. From Pattaya south towards Rayong, by way of the 10-km-long Jomtien Beach, lie a string of restaurants, resorts and small fishing villages which make the entire east coast a tourist's paradise.

Right: View from the Royal Cliff Beach Hotel, Pattaya.

PATTAYA AND HUA HIN are just about as different as two Thai seaside resorts can be. Pattaya is justly famous for its dynamic nightlife, and water-sports such as jet-skiing, para-sailing and diving. It's a relatively new resort, and unashamedly brash. Hua Hin, by contrast, is Thailand's oldest beach resort—quiet, laid-back and rather aristocratic. Both destinations are renowned for their seafood restaurants, but if you want to party all night then Pattaya is the place to be. In Hua Hin, just lie back under a palm tree and watch the stars.

pattaya &
hua hin

Two of Thailand's premier beach resorts, on opposite sides of the Bight of Bangkok, offer visitors great recreation and entertainment.

Clockwise from top left: The garden of the venerable Hua Hin Railway Hotel—now renamed the Sofitel Central, though just about everyone still calls it by its former name. Beach-side terrace leading to the Rama VI Royal Palace at Hua Hin. Winding down with a little relaxing Thai massage. Stylish bungalow accommodation available at Hua Hin.

phuket
& phang-nga bay

Phuket is a clear contender for the title "loveliest tropical island in the world", while the unusual karst formations of nearby Phang-nga Bay make an exciting and unique day trip.

Facing page: View of the Andaman Sea from Nai Han Beach in the island's deep south.

Clockwise from top: Soaking up the sun at Bang Tao Beach. View from the terrace of the Boat House Hotel at Kata Beach. Making a selection from the stunning buffet at Kata Beach's Club Med. Traditional sailing boat and luxury yacht in the pristine waters off Nai Han.

Phuket is a wonderful island where Thai culture meets the Malay world—the very name Phuket is derived from the Malay *bukit*, or hill. Here the visitor will find enchanting Sino-Portuguese architecture, a palm-fringed skyline studded with Buddhist temples and Muslim minarets, and some of the loveliest beaches in the world. As well as Thai, Chinese, Indian and Malay cuisine, world-class European and Japanese restaurants proliferate. In the south of the island the indigenous *chao tha-lae,* or "sea people" complete Phuket's intriguing ethnic mix. Busy Patong Beach is where most of the hotels, infrastructure and nightlife can be found.

Phang-nga Bay, lying just under 100 km northeast of Phuket, is an extraordinary expanse of turquoise sea studded with hundreds of tiny islands and sea stacks, mostly uninhabited, which are riddled with hidden passages, secret lagoons and submarine caves. Now a national park, the area can be explored by tour boat, canoe or—most excitingly—by sea kayak which allows the intrepid to enter the narrowest caves and grottoes. Visitors can call in for lunch at an enchanting Muslim fishing village, complete with mosque, which is perched on stilts. Nearby is the strangely-shaped "James Bond" Island, made world-famous by the movie *The Man with the Golden Gun.*

Clockwise from above:
Diver surveying a school of blue-striped snapper on a reef off Phuket.
Tourists relaxing on a converted Chinese junk sail the azure waters of the Andaman Sea.
Unloading fresh fish at a dockside in southern Phuket.

Clockwise from top: The extraordinary limestone outcrop known as "James Bond Island" in Phang-nga Bay. Visitors exploring the waters and limestone outcrops at Phang-nga. Aerial view of the coast and islands near Phang-nga.

Although less well-known than the nearby holiday island of Phuket, the magical beaches and forested cliffs of Krabi Province are rapidly being discovered.

krabi

Clockwise from right:
The elegant Dusit Rayavadee Resort at Phra Nang Bay.
Rock-climbing at Rai Leh Beach can be an exhilarating experience, but only for those with a head for heights!
Aboard a luxury yacht in the Andaman Sea off Rai Leh Beach.
Krabi's magnificent Ao Phra Nang Beach seen from the mouth of "Princess Cave".

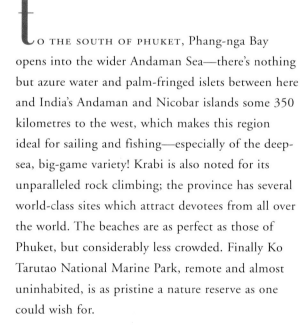

t O THE SOUTH OF PHUKET, Phang-nga Bay opens into the wider Andaman Sea—there's nothing but azure water and palm-fringed islets between here and India's Andaman and Nicobar islands some 350 kilometres to the west, which makes this region ideal for sailing and fishing—especially of the deep-sea, big-game variety! Krabi is also noted for its unparalleled rock climbing; the province has several world-class sites which attract devotees from all over the world. The beaches are as perfect as those of Phuket, but considerably less crowded. Finally Ko Tarutao National Marine Park, remote and almost uninhabited, is as pristine a nature reserve as one could wish for.

ko phi

After Phuket, Ko Phi Phi is the most popular destination on the Andaman Coast. It offers pristine beaches, impressive cliffs, clear water and fascinating marine life.

phi

Clockwise from top left of facing page: The azure waters around Ko Phi Phi contrast vividly with the verdant green of the islands themselves. A tranquil scene in the shallows of Phi Phi Don. Daredevil locals climbing improvised scaffolding to collect swallows' nests—the valuable raw material for birds' nest soup. The palm-covered, narrow strip of land linking the two halves of Phi Phi Don.

Ko phi phi consists of two islands—Phi Phi Don and Phi Phi Leh. It takes about two hours by boat to reach the islands, which are equidistant from Phuket and Krabi. The most popular destination is Phi Phi Don, which is almost two islands joined by a narrow finger of white coral sand forming a narrow, palm-covered isthmus. The swimming and diving offered in the area are unrivalled, and fresh seafood is readily available and extraordinarily fresh. For the present, the few islanders permanently resident on Phi Phi Don—including a few *chao thalae,* or "sea people"—remain friendly if a little shy.

ko samui

Like a jewel set in the tranquil waters of the Gulf of Thailand, Ko Samui is famed for the quality of its fruit and coconuts, the friendliness of its people, and the beauty of its unspoiled tropical scenery.

Facing page: Fishing boats in Bang Rak Bay off the northern coast of Ko Samui.
A Western tourist sleeping beneath a shady palm frond on Lamai Beach.
Left: Ko Samui's "Big Buddha" temple—known in Thai as Wat Phra Yai—looms above fishing boats anchored in Bang Rak Bay.
Middle, left: Looking out to sea across a garland of emerald islets; the central part of Ko Samui is quite mountainous and offers many splendid views.

Middle, right: Before tourism, the *chao Samui* or people of Samui made their living by exporting coconuts. Even today, the island is a sea of coconut palms.
Bottom: Waves breaking against a rocky outcrop on a deserted section of the southern coast of the island.

t HE COCONUT-PRODUCING ISLAND of Ko Samui was first "discovered" by backpackers in the 1970s and soon acquired a legendary status among travellers. Today it has moved considerably upmarket, and the island's many beaches are dotted with first-class hotels as well as more reasonably priced accommodation. It's a magical place by day, with crystal-clear waters and crisp, white beaches for sunbathing—but it's still more magical at night, as the island's large fleet of fishing boats puts to sea and illumines the horizons with coconut-oil fishing lamps. Samui is Thailand's second largest island after Phuket.

chiang mai

Above: Part of the elaborate gilded stupa at Wat Prathat Doi Suthep, symbol of Chiang Mai, which nestles half way up Doi Suthep, the mountain that dominates the city.
Left: Wat Phrathat Doi Suthep seen from higher up Doi Suthep.

tHAIS THINK OF SUKHOTHAI as the first independent Thai kingdom, but in fact Chiang Mai, the capital of the ancient Thai kingdom of Lan Na, or "One Million Rice Fields", is almost the same age. Recently the city celebrated its 700th anniversary with considerable style, an event that encouraged the Khon Muang, or people of the north, in the celebration of their ancient and sophisticated culture, which is quite distinct from that of Bangkok. Thais from other parts of the country love Chiang Mai,

Long celebrated as Thailand's "Rose of the North", Chiang Mai remains the most beautiful, elegant and historically interesting city in the country.

Left: Gilded Buddhas at Wat Chiang Man, the oldest temple in the city, founded by King Mangrai in the 13th century.
Below: Old spires at a new temple building at Wat Jet Yot, the venerable 15th-century temple where the 8th World Buddhist Council was convened in 1477.

Clockwise from top: Purple-coloured Vanda hybrid orchids. Colourful flowers decorate the verandah of a private house in the Mae Sa Valley just north of Chiang Mai.
The carefully manicured grounds of Chiang Mai's Lanna Resort Hotel.
Luxurious northern-style bungalows in the grounds of the Chiang Mai Regent Hotel.
Facing page: A house in the hills above Chiang Mai. Elephants with their mahouts put on a show at the Mae Sa Valley Elephant Camp.

regarding it both as a sort of Shangri La hidden in the northern hills, and as a very cold place. In fact it isn't cold except for a few weeks in December and January, but it's never as hot or humid as the central plains and Bangkok.

Chiang Mai, like all the major towns of the north, lies in a valley surrounded by wooded hills of great beauty. Here, where temperatures in January sometimes drop almost to freezing, there flourishes a very different ecosystem to that of the central plains. Orchids, staghorn ferns and huge vines hang from the trees, while waterfalls rush in torrents to join rivers leading in three separate directions—via the Salween to the Bay of Bengal, the Chao Phraya to the Gulf of Thailand, and the Mekong to the South China Sea. It's a naturalist's paradise, where trekkers can lose sight of the hustle and bustle of modern life for days at a time.

By any standards, Thailand is a cultured place—

Right: Chiang Mai girls in northern dress influenced by the Tai Lu minority hailing originally from southern Yunnan, China.
Below: Northern folk dance at a Buddhist temple.
Facing page: Umbrellas set out to dry in the sun at the umbrella-making village of Baw Sang near Chiang Mai.

yet even most Thais would agree that the most creative part of the country, which produces the best wood carvings and ceramics, the most diverse handicrafts (and, incidentally, is reputedly home to the prettiest women) is the north. All round the ancient city of Chiang Mai may be found "craft villages" producing everything from brightly-coloured umbrellas and elaborately-carved furniture to finely-woven silk and fine silver jewellery. Part of the reason for this creativity is the historically rich culture of the north, drawing as it does on the neighbouring traditions of Myanmar, Yunnan and Laos. Yet the collective whole is very special and uniquely northern Thai. Almost without exception visitors to the north, whether from Bangkok or abroad, return loaded with purchases. One of the outstanding sights of Chiang Mai, and perhaps the best place to make many of these purchases, is the northern capital's famed Night Bazaar.

Right: Potter at work in a craft village near Chiang Mai.
Far right: Chiang Mai girl applying coats of lacquer to skillfully crafted figurines.
Below: A woodcarver at work in the craft village of Ban Tawai near Chiang Mai.

lampang

Lampang is north Thailand's second city, with a rich cultural tradition of its own and perhaps the most spectacular Buddhist temples in the country—yet it receives relatively few visitors.

LAMPANG, KNOWN TO THE THAIS as *muang rot maa* or "pony cart city" because it is the last town in Thailand to employ this form of transport, is an old city founded during the 7th-century Dvaravati period. Nothing remains from these early times, but the city is rich in temples, many of which have a distinctly Burmese flavour. Lampang had a substantial Burmese population in the 19th century, most of whom were involved in the logging industry. At nearby Koka District is one of the

architectural wonders of Thailand, Wat Phra That Lampang Luang. Dating from around 1475, this temple is the most magnificent and best preserved example of northern Thai temple architecture.

Today Lampang is a modern city of shophouses and supermarkets, but the area to the north of the River Wang, which flows through the centre of town, retains an attractive 19th-century charm and is well worth a visit.

Top: Detail of mural, Wat Pong Yang Kok.

Above: A man of Lampang wrapped to protect himself against the sun—Thais value white skin.

Right: Celebrations at Lampang during the Wiang Lakon Festival.

Bottom: A secret—perhaps a compliment—passes between a Lampang man and woman, both wearing traditional northern garb.

Far left: The Burmese-style eaves of Lampang's Wat Si Chum.

Left: The richly ornate roof of Wat Pongsanuk Tai.

Below: Worshippers listen to a sermon at Wat Phra That Lampang Luang.

hill tribes of the
golden
triangle

Left: Red Lahu at a village in Chiang Rai Province.
Right: Poppy fields are still sometimes found in remote hill regions, but Thai opium production is negligible compared with that of neighbouring Myanmar and Laos.
Below: Dusk over the hills of the Golden Triangle.

For several centuries hill peoples from southern China and Tibet have wandered south to settle in the hills of northern Thailand.

Above, right: A young Karen girl in her traditional finery.
Above: A young Akha girl sporting a characteristic silver headdress.

$\mathcal{A}$LTHOUGH NUMBERING less than one per cent of the total population of Thailand, the *chao khao* or "people of the hills" constitute a particularly colourful and unusual element of the north. While Thais have traditionally settled in the valleys where they can practise their preferred culture of wet-rice paddy cultivation, the people of the hills prefer the sparsely-inhabited uplands where they grow dry rice, vegetables and—most notoriously—opium. In fact, very little illicit opium is grown in Thailand today, and many government projects, often initiated by the Thai royal family, exist to encourage the production of substitute crops such as fruit, temperate vegetables and tea.

It may seem confusing at first sight, but it doesn't take long to learn to distinguish the main hill tribes from each other by means of their traditional clothing. Akha women, for example, sport heavy silver headdresses; Yao women favour red boas; the Hmong are distinguished by their elaborately embroidered clothing, and the Lisu by their silver-studded waistcoats and elaborate silver neck-laces. Interestingly, it is almost always the women who follow tribal custom and wear traditional clothing—many of the men, from whichever hill tribe, prefer to wear ordinary, everyday clothing (particularly when in town) and are much harder to distinguish than their womenfolk.

Top: Lisu man playing a musical instrument.
Above: Detail of Lahu dress.
Right: Young Lahu boy holding his mother's hand at a market in Fang.

Above: Lisu people celebrating New Year at a village in Chiang Rai.

Left: Padaung "long neck" woman from Mae Hong Son. The Padaung are recent refugees from nearby Myanmar.

Far left: Yao women sporting distinctive red boas play with a small child at their village near Chiang Rai.

Below: Smiling Hmong girl at the Chiang Mai Night Bazaar.

mae hong son

Once known to officials as "Thailand's Siberia" because of its remoteness, Mae Hong Son is a delightful, tranquil retreat now easily reached by regular flights from Chiang Mai.

Founded in the mid-19th century as an elephant camp, Mae Hong Son has grown into a charming little wooden town complete with an attractive lake, several traditional Burmese-style temples and two first-class luxury hotels. Although very much a part of Thailand, few of the permanent residents except teachers and officials are in fact ethnic Thais. The great majority of the people of Mae Hong Son are Shan, Chinese Haw, Karen and other tribespeople, as well as Indians and Burmese hailing from across the nearby frontier with Myanmar.

Facing page: A supplicant nun at Mae Hong Son's Burmese-style Wat Doi Khong Mu.
Top left: Burmese influence is clearly apparent in the elaborately tiered eaves of Wat Hua Wiang.
Top right: A pious believer has applied gold leaf to this stone image of the Buddha at Mae Hong Son.
Above: Celebrants at Mae Hong Son's Muang Sam Mok Fair.
Right: Temple lights reflected in the placid waters of Jong Kham Lake, Mae Hong Son.

the great
northe

The broad plateau of northeast Thailand, traditionally the poorest part of the country, is also known as "The Green Northeast".

Northeast Thailand—known in Thai as Isaan—is a huge area of low rainfall and relatively unproductive land. It's also populated almost completely by Lao-speaking people, close kin to the population of neighbouring Laos, whilst there are also Khmer speakers around Buriram and Surin near the Cambodian frontier. In fact there are five times as many Lao in Isaan as there are in Laos, and since they form the backbone of the migrant labour force in Bangkok, there are almost certainly more Lao in the Thai capital than in the whole of Laos too. The

Facing page, top: Prasat Hin Phimai, near Khorat, is one of the finest examples of Khmer architecture outside Cambodia.
Facing page, bottom: The mighty Mekong River, which flows through the northeast, provides a vital lifeline for its people.
Left: Isaan girl sitting behind stone balusters at the ancient Khmer temple of Muang Tham.
Below: Treescape at Phu Kradung National Park, Loei.

Lao of Isaan are famous nationwide for their hospitality, sense of fun, distinctive spicy cuisine and homespun, country-style music.

Relatively few outsiders, whether Thai or foreign, visit the Northeast—though this looks set to change. Leaving aside the legendary hospitality of its people, the area is astonishingly rich in ancient Khmer architecture, and a "Khmer Culture Trail" runs from Phimai, near Khorat, all the way to Khao Phra Viharn, a dazzling hill-top sanctuary that lies just within Cambodia, but is accessible only from Thailand. Another excellent reason for visiting Isaan is that this is the home of *mat-mii* tie-dyed silk, a skill rediscovered by the American entrepreneur Jim Thompson and now famous worldwide.

Facing page: Isaan woman with flowers enters the ancient Khmer hill-top sanctuary of Prasat Hin Phanom Rung.
Clockwise from top:
Elephants at a village in Surin, site of the great annual Surin Elephant Round-up.
An Isaan grandmother, watched by her granddaughter, spins silk near Roi Et.
Details of silk textiles from the Northeast.
That Phanom, by the banks of the Mekong in the eastern-most part of Thailand, is revered as the symbol of Isaan.
Smiling Isaan girl.

Thailand is justly famous for its delicious food which, although almost unknown outside the country two decades ago, has now achieved recognition as a world-class cuisine among discerning diners just about everywhere.

thai food

Facing page, top: A dining room at the elegant Dusit Thani Hotel, Bangkok.
Facing page, bottom: *Luk jeeb*—Thai sweets fashioned to look like fruits.
Clockwise from top: *Tom yam kung*—prawn and lemon grass soup with mushrooms—and *tod man pla*—Thai fish fritters.

A display of Thai food in traditional *benjarong* ceramic dishes.
Pan-fried snapper with kaffir-lime leaves, cashew nuts and chopped onion and ginger garnish—a southern speciality.
Stylishly-sculpted fresh fruits; for Thais, food presentation is an art form.

HAI RESTAURANTS are springing up in cities all over the world, and they offer delicious fare. But this cannot really prepare the visitor for the unexpectedly wide range of temptingly exotic tastes available in the kingdom itself. For one thing, there are four main regional cuisines. There's the cooking of Bangkok and the Central Plains, which is what is generally served at restaurants abroad. Beyond this there is the simpler, spicy fare of the northeast, specialising in dishes like *somtam* papaya salad and *kai yang* grilled chicken; then there's the rather hotter, seafood-oriented cooking of the peninsular south, and finally the rich, rather heavier cooking of the north, influenced by neighbouring Myanmar and Yunnan. They're all delicious—and none of them have to be too spicy-hot. Just tell your Thai hosts: *mai chop phet*—I don't like it spicy!

It's not just the variety of dishes and flavours that stuns the visitor to Thailand and ensures that most people will return again and again; it's the sheer

number of places serving food, from restaurants as elegant as any in London, Paris or New York, through exquisitely-set *suan ahaan*, or "garden restaurants", to hole-in-the-wall cafés and night markets served by ranks of *rot kaen*, or mobile food carts. It seems an unlikely claim, but it's true. Wherever you eat, at whatever price level, the food is generally delicious, fresh and clean. It's also the original land of "service with a smile"!

Food in Thailand is generally accompanied by rice—long grain in the centre and south, quite often

Top left: Dried squid vendor with his *rot kaen*, or mobile food cart.
Top right: Preparing noodles at a mobile food shop that can be carried in its entirety on a shoulder pole.
Above: Preparing a dish of broad *kuaytiaw* noodles and fresh seafood.
Right: A tempting display of coconut-based Thai sweets.

Above: The range of spices and condiments used in Thai cooking is wonderful. Those seen here—capsicum and chilli peppers, coriander, cumin, galingale, ginger, kaffir limes, fresh green pepper vine, lemon grass and *makrut* leaves—represent just a small sample.
Far left: Fruit and vegetables kept fresh by a trickle of water from a bamboo pipe.
Left: A pile of juicy fresh rambutan.

sticky glutinous rice in the north and the northeast. Thais eat with a spoon and fork. Only Chinese dishes are eaten with chopsticks. All dishes are served at the same time, and the correct etiquette is to take a small amount of whatever you desire from the communal dishes using a serving spoon provided, and place this on your own plate with rice. Thais consider eating to be both a serious business and great fun—they hate to eat alone, so expect to be invited to sit down and join in meals on a regular basis.

thai crafts

The skills of Thailand's craft workers are legendary, and their products models of sophistication and good taste.

Top: The elegant living room of Jim Thompson's House in Bangkok.
Above: Lacquered tables and containers once used for betel nut equipment.
Right: An elaborate *khon* mask used in classical Thai dancing.

tHAILAND HAS A LONG TRADITION of sophisticated arts and crafts, based originally on the
labours of craftsmen and women at the royal courts
of Sukhothai, Chiang Mai, Ayutthaya and—most
recently—Bangkok. The dexterity of the workers,
and the elegance of their products, be it in precious
metals, wood, lacquer, paper or stone, has to be seen
to be believed. And while genuine antiques are
expensive and generally require an export permit,
today's craft workers, the descendants of many
skilled generations before them, can produce near-
perfect copies of antiquities with as great success as
they can create new, modern designs.

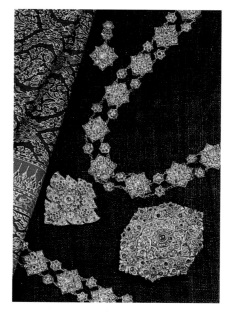

Top left: Silver betel
containers, an elegantly carved
table and a gilded screen at
the Sukhothai Hotel, Bangkok.
Top right: Traditional
mulberry-paper folding
manuscript with religious
paintings and text.
Above, left: Nielloware vessels
piled high at an upmarket
Bangkok restaurant.
Above, right: Detail of gilded
painting on black lacquer at
Bangkok's Oriental Hotel.
Left: Elegant, hand-wrought
jewellery dating from the
19th century.

visiting thailand

Thai hospitality is legendary.
Wherever you go you're
certain to be made welcome.

iT'S EASY TO VISIT THAILAND. The kingdom
has international airports at Bangkok, Chiang Mai
and Phuket. The choice of accommodation is aston-
ishing—there's everything from super-luxury world
class hotels like the Oriental and the Shangri-La in
Bangkok, through the modern Thai-style Regent
Resort in Chiang Mai, to friendly, reasonably priced
guesthouses. The same is true of dining—it seems
that everywhere you turn there are restaurants
offering mouth-watering cuisine. Be prepared for
an amazing culinary choice.

Facing page, top: The luxurious lobby of Bangkok's Sukhothai Hotel.

Facing page, bottom left: Looking down on a swimming pool at the Royal Orchid Sheraton Hotel, Bangkok.

Facing page, bottom right: Arranging flowers at a Bangkok restaurant.

Left: The Amanpuri resort in Phuket offers traditional Thai architecture as well as incredible luxury and peace.

Below: Illuminated stage in a pool at the Sukhothai Hotel.

Bottom: All the comforts of home—and usually more. A typical Thai hotel room.

Front cover, top to bottom:
Floating market; a Thai woman gives the traditional *wai* greeting; Wat Phra Kaew, Bangkok.

Back cover, top to bottom:
Temple carving detail; Thai *khon* mask; relaxing on a beach in Krabi; Thailand has many beautiful beaches like this one on Krabi.

Published by Periplus Editions (HK) Ltd., with editorial office at 130 Joo Seng Road #06-01, Singapore 368357.

Copyright © 2000 Periplus Editions (HK) Ltd.

All rights reserved. No part of this publication may be reproduced or utilized in any form or by any means, electronic or mechanical, including photocopying, recording, or by any information storage and retrieval system, without prior written permission from the publisher.

ISBN-13 978-962-593-211-8
ISBN-10 962-593-211-9

Writer: Andrew Forbes

Distributed by:
Asia Pacific
Berkeley Books Pte. Ltd.
130 Joo Seng Road #06-01
Singapore 368357
Tel: (65) 6280-1330
Fax: (65) 6280-6290
inquiries@periplus.com.sg
www.periplus.com

North America, Latin America & Europe
Tuttle Publishing
364 Innovation Drive
North Clarendon, VT 05759-9436 U.S.A.
Tel: 1 (802) 773-8930
Fax: 1 (802) 773-6993
info@tuttlepublishing.com
www.tuttlepublishing.com

First edition
10 09 08 07 06   10 9 8 7 6 5 4 3 2

Printed in Singapore

Photographic Credits

All photographs by **Photobank**, except:

Beck, Josef, pp 22 (top), 32 (main photo, bottom), 35 (bottom)
Dallas & John Heaton, p 24 (bottom)
Dugast, Jean-Léo, pp 9 (middle), 11 (third from bottom)
Evrard, Alain, p 47 (middle right)
Gottschalk, Manfred, p 35 (middle right)
Nacivet, Jean, p. 34 (bottom)
Noirot, Didier, p 28 (top right)
Strange, Rick, p. 55 (bottom)
Wassman, Bill, pp 9 (middle), 49 (bottom right), 54